Marstella

A Day in the Life of a Sea Star

A non-fiction book about sea stars through the voice of a fictional character named Marstella.

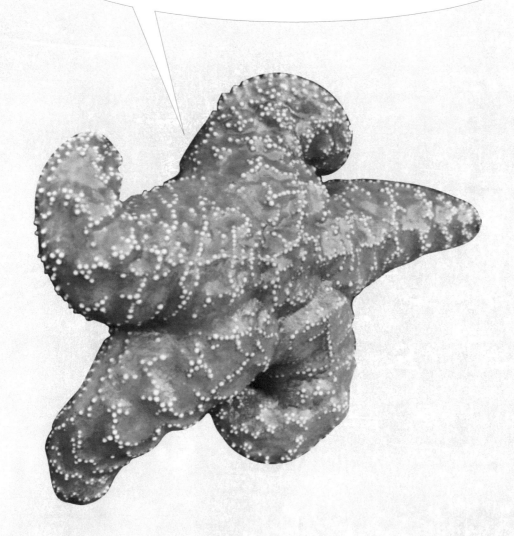

Ochre Sea Star
(Pisaster ochraceus)

Sea stars are in a category
of ocean animals called
Echinoderms (eh-KI-no-derms),
which means spiny skins.

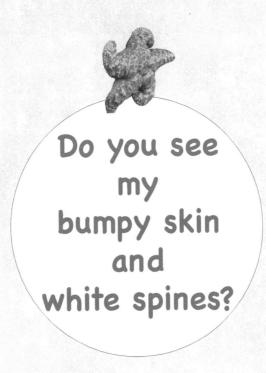

Do you see
my
bumpy skin
and
white spines?

I have lots of friends.
Do you want to meet
my BFFs?

Sharna

Ochre Sea Star
(Pisaster ochraceus)

Batray

Bat Star
(Patiria miniata)

Estrella

Ochre Sea Star
(Pisaster ochraceus)

Shiuda

Pink Sea Star
(Pisaster brevispinus)

No matter
what our differences may be,
we all get along.

There are about
2,000 kinds
of sea stars in the world.

Sea stars come in many
colors, sizes, and shapes.

My friends and I live in the Pacific Ocean, in Northern California, but our relatives can be found in all the oceans of the world.

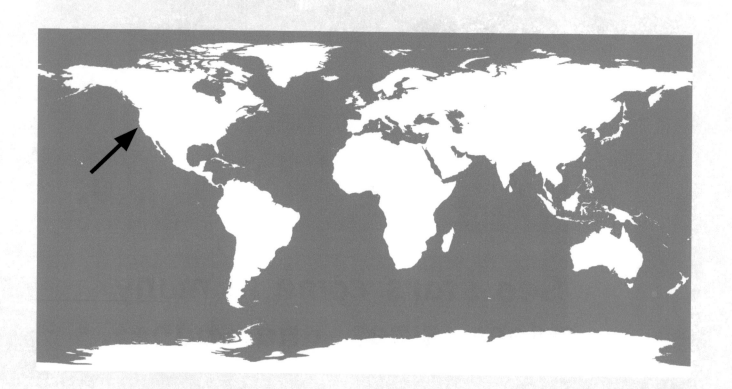

Sea stars can be found in
cold or warm water.

They can be found in
deep or shallow water.

Our tops and bottoms
look different, but our
lefts and our rights look the same!

Sea stars are fairly symmetrical, meaning that each
half looks about the same as the other half.

Most sea stars have
five arms (rays)
around a circular middle.

In some parts of the world,
sea stars have
40 to 50 arms.

DON'T CALL US FISH!

People sometimes call
sea stars, starfish,
but they are
NOT fish.

Sea stars are
invertebrates.
Invertebrates do not have
backbones.

Come on, friends!
Let's climb!

Some sea stars have thousands of tiny tube feet on each arm.

Feet

These feet help sea stars cling to the rocks.

I love doing a good yoga stretch!

Sea stars don't move
very fast or far,
unless carried by the waves.

One arm often leads
and the other arms follow.

I'm hungry!
I think I will join my
friends for lunch.

18

Sea stars eat mussels, shrimp, other small shellfish, barnacles, sea urchins, worms, and algae.

Can you quickly say this tongue twister "muscling mussels" five times?

Sea stars' feet help pull shells apart.

Sea stars have a two-part stomach.

One part comes out of the body to start eating.

Hide and Seek time!
Can you find me?

22

Sea stars can be seen in intertidal zones.

Intertidal zones are the areas between low tide and high tide.

Sea stars depend on the sea water returning with high tide.

 I'm so thirsty!
I hope high tide comes
in soon!

Madreporite
It often looks like an orange or light dot.

Sea stars let in
sea water through a
topside filter.

It is called a
madreporite (mah-druh-poor-Ite).

Water then flows
through channels in
the sea stars' bodies.

Let's play in this cave!

Sea stars are safer
from predators
when hidden from sight.

Predators include
birds, crabs, otters, snails,
large fish, and humans!

Can you find the eyespots
on my friend?

Sea stars have eye spots on
the tip of
each arm.

The eye spots help
sea stars sense
what types of objects are
around them.

This helps them find food
and avoid danger.

 Time for our daily growth mindset practice!

Sea stars can grow back missing arms, which is called regeneration.

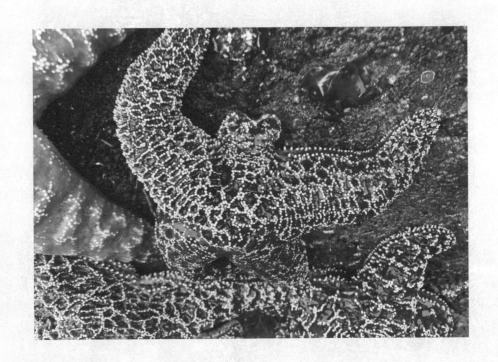

It takes about a year for an arm to grow back.

Do you want to
join our
sea star party?

A group of sea stars is called a constellation or a galaxy.

Please come enjoy us
with your eye spots!